Teaching Self-Control
in the classroom - a
Cognitive Behavioural Approach

by

Patricia Gourley

Illustrated by
Philippa Drakeford

Acknowledgements

I would like to thank the following people who assisted me in so many ways with this publication:

- Harry Rafferty for his help in forming my ideas into a research project and his guidance in its implementation.

- Michael Stewart who assisted with the statistical analysis.

- Jo Matchett, friend and colleague, who worked so diligently on the initial research programme.

- Martin McGlade and the staff and pupils of Harberton School, Belfast.

- My family and friends who offered support and diversion at all the right times.

Contents

Section 1 - Learning and Practising
Weeks 1 - 7: Copiable Story Sheets and Activities

Section 2 - Application
 Weeks 8 - 12: Copiable Workbook and Goal Sheets

Background

My interest in Cognitive Behavioural Therapy (CBT) arose from a number of different sources. One was my experience of classroom management as a class teacher. During my four years of work as a teacher in a Special School for children with moderate learning difficulties, I used a range of behaviour modification techniques with my classes of children aged between seven and eight. I found these very effective but was unhappy with them for two reasons: I found them time consuming to manage and I also had reservations about their educational validity.

To counter the teacher intensive monitoring that they required I began to involve the pupils in the self-monitoring and self-evaluation of their own behaviours. I was surprised at how successful this turned out to be and, in addition, it also went some way to addressing my second reservation. In traditional behaviour modification it appeared to me that children were not really learning about controlling their own behaviour, rather they were performing to an agenda set by an external source. Ethically I felt that I wanted to impart some self-management skills to pupils and this appeared to be more possible when students became involved themselves.

Whilst examining possible research topics for my MSc in Developmental and Educational Psychology my interest was considerably influenced by Tammie Ronen's book, "Cognitive Developmental Therapy with Young Children." Ronen argued that even young children can benefit from self-control training and that it is a useful tool for managing behaviour in the classroom. I realised that I had been using some CBT techniques with my former classes and I agreed, through personal experience, with both claims. I became aware of the arguments for not following CBT with young children due to their developmental limitations, and yet even my limited experience showed that it was possible.

On the basis of this experience, I was interested to see whether a fully structured self-control training programme, based on CBT would be of any use to the pupils I had been teaching previously who were both young and had limited educational ability. I decided that the best approach would be to develop a self-control training programme based on Ronen and Wozner's model (1995), carry it out with a whole class at the Special School at which I had previously taught, and evaluate its effectiveness. My purpose for undertaking the study was to see if young children with learning difficulties would benefit from self control training. The results were very successful, showing that it had a highly significant effect on children's on-task behaviour in the classroom.

The format of the programme has since been altered and developed so that it can be used by teachers in the mainstream primary classroom who may have no knowledge of cognitive behavioural therapy and its techniques. In my current work as an educational psychologist I have used aspects of the programme with groups of children exhibiting high-frequency, low-level behaviours and have attempted to pass on the skills to their teachers. So far the results have been encouraging. Learning, in a non-critical way, about the relationship between thoughts and behaviour appears to be novel, stimulating and enjoyable for the children. Involving them in their own behaviour change seems to increase motivation and self-confidence.

This programme is only one way of developing self-control in children aged between 7-11. Although CBT has fundamental tenets, rationale and basic techniques, the way these are presented to the young child is open to change depending on the individual. No doubt I will be adapting aspects of it as my experiences introduce more effective stories, analogies and examples for imparting self-control skills. I hope that teachers feel free to do the same.

Introduction

If pupils are to become self-motivated, independent learners capable of exercising the skills of self-discipline and responsibility required of them (Elton 1990), then self-control training would appear to be a prerequisite. Many teachers and parents see the ability of a child to develop self-control as a main target of education; as children acquire self-control they become better able to behave appropriately, restrain and stop unwanted actions, overcome difficulties and postpone immediate gratification (Kendall and Braswell 1985). Cooper and Upton, (1991) argue that pupils do not require external control, instead they should be encouraged to take part in the decision making that moulds their lives. The aim of self control training is to develop a sense of mastery (Kendall 1993), so that the individual is not driven by impulsive or limiting thoughts, and thus has the ability to shape their own life.

This book is based on Ronen and Wozner's cognitive developmental model (1995) for imparting self-control in children. It is based on cognitive behavioural therapy and uses a developmental framework within which to develop cognitive skills. Ronen and Wozner claim that this model is an effective method of developing self-control in children who, previously, have been considered too young to gain from cognitive therapy.

The introduction section will examine cognitive behavioural therapy (CBT) from a historical perspective, briefly reviewing its roots in both cognitive therapy and behaviour therapy and highlighting techniques most commonly used with children. The development of CBT in schools shall be examined and the reasons why it is an appropriate method of dealing with behaviour problems will be explored. Finally, the developmental considerations that need to be taken into account when using self-control training with young children will be discussed.

The following section will contain the teaching materials, lesson notes and resources designed to impart self-control techniques to young children in the classroom. These lessons have been developed from those that were used in my original research project and although similar in content, presentation has been revised to make them accessible to teachers who have no knowledge of CBT techniques.

Historical Perspective

Cognitive behavioural therapy (CBT) has been described as an umbrella term for different treatment techniques that can be offered in many different sequences and permutations. Ronen (1995). It is a combination of aspects of behaviour therapy and cognitive therapy which have been expanded

and refined for clinical use with the aim of modifying undesirable behaviour. The aspects of these therapies most commonly used in CBT are discussed below.

Behaviour Therapy

The behaviour therapy component has been heavily influenced by operant conditioning, taking many strategies from this field, although some classical conditioning applications are also used. Operant conditioning states that if a response is followed by a reward, the response is more likely to occur again. It is concerned with how behaviour is changed by its consequences. Applications commonly used with children include positive reinforcement, the use of primary and secondary reinforcers, behavioural contracts, contingency management and delay of reinforcement.

Some of the advantages claimed for operant conditioning strategies are that they are clear, concrete and easily understood and therefore accessible to children. Despite the effectiveness of these strategies drawbacks have been noted: Kadzin (1975) pointed out that the administration of rewards may lead to a situation where the performance of target behaviours are restricted to the presence of particular cues. Also, there may be difficulties in generalising skills to situations where externally administered rewards have not been applied.

Modelling, another behavioural technique, is used within CBT and has been found to be successful when used with children to teach them to cope with anxiety, stress, instilling social skills and teaching children to intercept automatic thoughts.

Cognitive Therapy

Cognitive therapy assumes that an individual's behaviour is largely determined by the way s/he perceives and makes sense of the world (Kendall 1993). Schemata (Beck 1963), are attitudes and assumptions about the world based on previous experience. These schemata are considered as important links in the chain of events leading to disordered behaviour (Powell and Oei 1991).

The influence of using thoughts and emotions to alter behaviour was highlighted when Albert Ellis (1962) examined their role in the treatment of neurosis. Ellis advocated clients to examine the rationality of their beliefs using this as a primary mechanism for the modification of distorted thoughts. Treatment involved verbal persuasion, argument and questioning.

Beck's (1963) method, in the treatment of depression, was based more on exploring the individual's unique meaning systems. In his therapeutic approach Beck aimed to help clients to become experienced in the necessary skills for examining and testing their own beliefs by introducing the monitoring and recording of behaviour and using positive self talk to alter one's thoughts.

Michenbaum's (1979) approach united the restructuring of thoughts, behavioural self-management techniques and training in verbal self-instruction. He emphasised the self-statement, changing present self-talk to positive self-talk, would facilitate change.

Zurilla's (Ronen 1994) focus was on problem-solving training which would provide a framework for dealing with problematic situations and would assist in decision making.

Bandura's work stressed the role of expectancies in human behaviour; as expectancies influence experience and vice versa so they act in reciprocal influence to affect outcome.

Cognitive-Behavioural Therapy

Although CBT encompasses facets of both these models only selective aspects are applied: CBT rejects both the traditional behaviourist view of behaviour as a function of the environment and the cognitive view of behaviour as a product of person variables (Kendall 1993). Instead, the cognitive behavioural model views personal variables, i.e., thoughts and feelings and the environment as forming a 'mutual influence system'.
Kendall states:

> *Cognitive therapy views changing behaviour alone as too narrowly focused; however in CBT the performance based feature is not eliminated. CBT focuses on how people respond to their cognitive interpretations of experiences rather than the environment or the experience itself and how thoughts and behaviours are related. It combines cognition change procedures with behavioural contingency management and learning experiences designed to help change distorted or deficient information processing.*

CBT could be said to be an attempt to unite aspects of behaviour therapy with the insights of cognitive therapy and, through this synthesis, create behaviour change.

CBT is based on the premise that personal problems occur due to irrational thinking and that the main cause of maladaptive behaviour is the connection between thoughts and emotions (Ronen 1997). A blend of cognitive and behavioural techniques are used to firstly raise awareness of the self and one's emotions, and secondly, to modify thought processes through a variety of strategies, including altering perceptions, attributions and expectations; initiating internal dialogue through positive self-talk and self-instruction; using self-monitoring and self-reward; and developing problem-solving skills. These techniques require the individual's active participation in changing thinking and altering behaviour.

Cognitive-Behavioural Techniques in Schools

Developing self-control in school children has long been viewed as an important factor in education. In the early seventies research on CBT moved from the clinical setting and into the classroom. Many of the CBT techniques used today are essentially the same as those developed then with only slight improvements and refinements.

1. Self-Instruction/Self-Talk
Michenbaum (1977) developed the verbal self-instructional model based on the premise that a teacher can instruct

students to work through a series of self-instructional steps to facilitate learning and problem solving. Here children are taught how to interrupt the chain of thoughts that lead to an automatic reaction by deliberately thinking or saying aloud a prerehearsed statement and/or visualising a series of images. This technique has been used in a variety of settings to include learning strategies, behaviour change and approaches to problems.

2. *Modelling*
Modelling is often used to reinforce and complement self-instructional training. Here the teacher or tutor acts out a series of steps concerning, for example, how to behave in an appropriate way. The teacher speaks aloud to herself as she proceeds through these steps whilst the child watches on. The child then copies the process, all the while talking aloud to himself and receiving feedback from the teacher. Eventually the talking aloud is faded to silent self-talk and the child is left with a practised strategy for approaching a certain problem.

3. *Self-Monitoring*
There is evidence from a variety of writers on the effectiveness of commonly used CBT techniques in schools, (Rosenbaum and Drabman, 1979). In studies where children were asked to monitor and control their own behaviour increases in appropriate behaviours occurred as the children began to develop insights into their own behaviour.

4. *Self-Evaluation*
Self-evaluation, where the child judges his own performance, (often against criteria such as school rules) was found, when paired with reinforcement, to result in decreases in disruptive behaviours.

5. *Reinforcement/Reward*
Research on the use of reward shows that the use of self-determined reinforcers are equally effective in promoting behaviour change as teacher-determined ones. Sheldon (1995) notes that the move from concrete rewards to using self-statements is an important element in developing self-control.

These cognitive-behavioural techniques have continued to be used within the school setting and, over time, have been expanded and refined to deal with a range of school-related behaviour and learning difficulties. These include, for example, fears and anxieties, hyperactivity and impulsivity, obedience and disruptive problems, developing problem solving skills and in teaching learning strategies to learning disabled children. CBT has also been used with children with ADHD although studies have found that it alone is not as effective as using it combined with medication (Kendall 1993).

The Appropriateness of CBT as a Technique for Behaviour Management

Self-control training using CBT is particularly appropriate for dealing with children's behaviour management problems for several reasons. Firstly, it works; an analysis of numerous studies where CBT was used Durlak, Fuhrman and Lampman (1991) found that overall it had a highly significant effect on changing behaviour for children aged between eleven and thirteen.

Secondly, it is a suitable technique for developing thinking skills that are deficient in children exhibiting problem behaviours. Forehand and Weirson (1993) state that if low self-control is interfering with developmental mastery then cognitive self-control is particularly important. It has been noted that children with deviant behaviour suffer from deficiencies in particular thought processes or from an inability to apply self-control skills.

Ronen (1991, 1997) lists a number of cognitive characteristics of the child displaying behaviour problems such as hyperactivity, impulsivity and aggression, which include:

- difficulties in inhibiting responses
- difficulties in taking others' perspectives
- misattribution of others' intentions
- difficulties in finding a connection between one's own behaviour and others' responses
- less sensitivity to interpersonal conflict
- lack of use of evaluative techniques and the inability to set criteria for evaluating their own behaviour
- inability to predict their own behaviour patterns, even those in the near future
- difficulties in planning actions
- emphasising ends or goals rather than intermediate steps
- difficulties in generating a range of alternative solutions.

As Ronen (1991) points out, these characteristics are directly connected to cognitive deficits or disorders and therefore cognitive therapy should be a natural treatment option.

Cognitive Behavioural Therapy with Primary aged Children

Although there is little debate over the value of developing self-control skills in school aged pupils there is some argument over whether it can be effectively developed in young children. Durlak et al.'s (1991) analysis of numerous studies using CBT interventions with children found that, for those aged under 11, their programmes gains were not as great as those for children aged over 11. However, recent research has shown that CBT can be used successfully with children under the age of 11 if the child's unique method of thinking is taken into account when delivering programmes (Ronen 1997). Forehand and Weirson (1995) state that the practice of borrowing from the adult's CBT model and applying it to children is inadequate in that it ignores developmental theory and has avoided adapting techniques to children's specific problems and characteristics as unique to those of adults. Several authors agree that children's cognitive functioning should be addressed when considering CBT treatments, (Kendall and Braswell 1985, Forehand and Weirson 1995).

Ronen (1991) argues that, although it is difficult for young children to understand the abstract concepts, rational thinking and verbal communication that cognitive therapy requires, this is no reason for limiting its usage with them. She points out that learning takes place in a number of ways; in the academic realm children's ability to learn complicated subjects from a very early age is well accepted. Therefore, why should this not be the case when applying cognitive therapy with children? Could it be that cognitive therapy is just not presented in an accessible way for children? From this standpoint it is incumbent on the teacher to design techniques that will appropriately meet the child's developmental needs.

So what are these developmental needs and how should they be addressed? Researchers isolate three main areas for consideration: cognitive processes, language, and method of intervention.

Cognitive Considerations

Egocentrism

It is important, when working with children, that adults should take into account their egocentrism (DiGuiseppe 1989). Therefore, the method of training should make reference to the child's own experiences with the use of demonstrations, metaphors and illustrations from their own lives (Ronen 1997).

Consequences

As children are often unaware that their behaviours, actions or emotions have a negative impact on their lives and as they do not usually recognise that there are alternative ways for them to act and think (DiGuiseppe 1989) then the programme should point out the consequences of behaviours and, through training, make other alternatives accessible.

Concrete Thinking
Because of young children's reliance on concrete thought, abstract terms should be translated into concrete ones, e.g., "automatic thought" becomes "doing something without thinking about it" (Ronen 1997), or "problem behaviours" becomes "things that you do that get you into trouble."

Visual Representation
As children rely heavily on visual representation then emphasis should be placed on the use of concrete and simple materials, e.g., pictures, diagrams and stories (DiGuiseppe 1989).

Fun
Use should be made of the child's natural capacity for imagination, games and play when delivering the programme (Ronen 1997).

Reference Groups
Traditionally, preadolescent children find adults in authority a significant reference for reinforcement therefore teachers should be incorporated into treatment (Forehand and Weirson 1995).

Language Considerations

Capacity for Self Talk
The use of language is central to CBT in imparting and facilitating self-control skills and in learning to use mediated thoughts (Ronen 1997). Children's capacity for talking aloud means that self-instruction can easily be practised.

Adaptation of Language
Several researchers have commented on the adaptation of language when delivering CBT programmes to young children (Kendall and Braswell 1985). It is important to change the language used to suit the child's level of development by using simple words and phrases, e.g. "mediated thought" becomes "an order that the brain sends the body" (Ronen 1994).

Classroom Considerations
In using CBT in schools it is important to adapt the procedures of intensive one-to-one interventions for use in the classroom. Ashman and Conway (1989) list the following characteristics that a programme must have for it to be an effective tool in whole class management of behaviour:
- there must be meaningful analysis of content and tasks for the learner
- it should require the active participation of the student

- behaviour management techniques should be used to maintain motivation
- teacher input should fade to promote self-initiated learning
- clear feedback is necessary
- strategies should be systematically introduced
- multiple training sessions are necessary
- emphasis should be placed on the value of strategies used
- extensive use should be made of strategy examples
- each stage of the training procedure should involve analysis and review.

Methods of Intervention

Ronen and Wozner's (1995) Self-Control Intervention Model

The self-control intervention model (Ronen and Wozner, 1995) proposes an educational therapeutic process comprising five phases which Ronen (1997) describes as follows:

Phase 1: Modification of maladaptive concepts
The purpose of this stage is to teach the child that the problem is a behaviour that is dependent on him or her and therefore can be altered if the child learns how to do so. Modification is achieved through cognitive restructuring and redefinition. Techniques used at this stage may consist of questioning and giving paradoxical examples to assist the child in realising that the behaviour is within their control.

Phase 2: Understanding the process of the problem
During the second phase the child is taught about the connection between his or her brain, body and problematic behaviour. Rational analysis of this process helps the child to understand how the problem has evolved and that they can take responsibility for it. Written materials, discussions, pictures and diagrams may be used at this stage.

Phase 3: Increasing awareness of internal stimuli

This stage is concerned with developing sensitivity in general and also to internal stimuli related to the specific problem through encouraging the child to concentrate on how they feel. The purpose is to help the child to recognise internal cues regarding their problem. Relaxation, concentration and monitoring are techniques that may be used.

Phase 4: Developing self-control

This is attained by teaching the child techniques for mediating their automatic behaviours. The child may be trained in physical as well as emotional exercises to develop their sense of self-control. Self-monitoring, self-evaluation, self-reinforcement, problem solving and imagination may be utilised here.

Phase 5: Elimination of the problem

At this stage the problem is decreased through monitoring, assessment, maintenance and working towards generalisation. Self-confidence and self-efficacy should develop.

Included in the five phases are three main components designed to consolidate the acquisition of self-control:

1. learning
2. practising
3. application.

In addition, the model is set within a theoretical framework comprising the following principles (Ronen 1997):

- teachers using cognitive-behavioural methods when working with children should allow for developmental and social differences in order to adapt programmes to match their needs
- the nature of the problem and the child's capacity will influence the intervention chosen
- it is inadequate to use direct adaptation of adult techniques for children. Specific techniques for children should address two unique features: children's irrational thinking and their need for a sense of enjoyment from the subject at hand
- interventions should be designed with a view to preventing problems and will help children's general adjustment and coping.

Ronen and Wozner's model for developing self control has been used in a range of applications but has mostly been used with individual children in clinical settings. Applications include problems such as sleep disorders (Ronen 1993), encopresis (Ronen 1993), nocturnal enuresis (Ronen, Wozner and Rahav, 1992), fears and anxieties (Ronen 1996) and trauma (Ronen 1996). The original model was adapted into an educational programme (Ronen 1994) aiming to impart self-control skills to eight and twelve year old schoolchildren.

The programme was composed of two parts incorporating firstly, learning and training in, and secondly, practise of, new knowledge on self-control at school. It was aimed at teaching young children self-help methods for controlling behaviour and decreasing aggression and obedience problems at school. The programme consisted of two stages and was mainly self-taught through the manuals the students received, one including theoretical material and the other consisting of homework assignments. The results of the evaluation showed that there was an increase in self-control ratings, (as measured by the Children's Self-Control Rating Scale, Rosenbaum and Ronen, 1991), in the eight year-old group.

My own research was developed within the same framework and contained similar teaching points however the method of transmission was through teacher-led, whole-class lessons with circle-time follow up sessions. Resources and stories also differed. Results showed that the programme had a highly significant effect on promoting on-task behaviour in the classroom.

The Programme

This programme is designed to teach self-control skills using cognitive behavioural therapy (CBT) to children with problems of low-level, high frequency behaviours. The target age is between seven and eleven.

Format

The programme consists of two main sections. The first section concerns learning and practising CBT skills while the second section allows these skills to be applied in the classroom environment.

Section 1- Learning and Practising

There are seven booklets. These are:
>   Looking at Behaviour
>   Deciding to Change
>   The Brain and the Body
>   Stopping and Thinking
>   Feelings and Beliefs
>   Recording and Rewarding
>   Starting to Change.

The booklets contain the bulk of the learning material. Material covered includes theoretical instruction in knowledge areas such as the body, the brain and automatic and mediated thoughts. A variety of techniques are also covered including self-monitoring, self-evaluation, self-reinforcement, self-instruction and guided imaging, all of which can be used as methods to change unwanted behaviour. The seven stories cover the main areas of Cognitive Behavioural Therapy in a manner designed to be accessible to children. Each book is accompanied by teaching notes which offer topics for discussion and follow-on activities where appropriate. A typical lesson would entail reading a book with the pupils and then following the teaching notes for discussion or the other activities. At some stage it may be necessary to augment the programme with further discussion or practice sessions depending on the pupils' understanding of the main principles.

It is anticipated that one booklet will be covered each week therefore this section will take seven weeks to complete.

Section 2 - Application

The lessons are followed by a period where the pupil is asked to carry out the skills learned in normal class time using the suggested record booklets. Weekly meetings should continue for the purpose of goal setting and evaluation. The time limit for this section is indefinite but four weeks of graded practise with teacher monitoring should be sufficient. Once the skills are learned teacher monitoring should be less frequent but progress should be discussed from time to time.

Group Size

There are various ways in which the material can be used.

Small Groups
This may be organised by a teacher who is interested in behaviour management or a special needs coordinator. The particpants may be drawn from different classes from within the school. The class teacher's participation would be necessary for the Application section of the programme.

Whole Class
It could be used in a whole class basis depending on class size and as long as all the class would have access to the teaching materials. The discussion sections may be more difficult with a whole class but could fit into already established circle-time sessions.

One-to-One
The programme may be used on a one-to-one basis but this would mean that peer support, which has been found to be a useful component of the programme, would not occur.

Duration

Weeks 1-7   Stories and Activities.
Weeks 8-12   Application, Goal Setting and Evaluation.

Each lesson should take between 30 to 60 minutes, depending on the number of pupils in the group and the length of the discussion. With one lesson occurring each week it would take at least seven weeks to cover the teaching and practice material and a further four weeks to cover the application section.

How to use the Programme

Section 1 - Learning and Practice

The Stories
The story booklets chart the progress of a group of children as they attempt to develop self-control skills with the help of their class teacher. The stories provide examples of self-control strategies, and how they can be practised and applied. They also form the basis of discussion periods where the pupils are encouraged to examine their own behaviour, self-perceptions and others' attitudes towards them.

The stories should be read by the teacher to the group or class. The teacher should ensure that all members have access to the text and illustrations which are an important aid to learning. They exist to represent complicated material in an understandable way and reinforce the main teaching points. The stories are printed ready to copy and staple. Some pupils might choose to follow the text as the teacher reads. Others, especially those with delayed reading skills, will listen and should be encouraged to look at the pictures when appropriate.

Discussion
At the end of the stories there are questions and points for discussion. These have a variety of roles whether enabling

identification with the main characters, recognising feelings, reflecting on personal behaviour or generating alternatives. It has also been found that through group interaction the major concepts and principles are reworded in the child's own language. This has been found to be an important component in assisting group understanding.

The teacher should lead the discussion, giving all group members the opportunity to contribute if so desired. It is important as the children disclose information (which they may be uncomfortable about) that this takes place in a friendly atmosphere where the dialogue emphasises acceptance and the potential for improvement.

Activities
The programme contains optional worksheets which exist to reinforce the main teaching points if necessary. In addition the pupils are given opportunities to practise self-control techniques ranging from physiological discrimination to self-monitoring and recording.

Summary of Lessons: Weeks 1 - 7

Story One - Looking at Behaviour
This introduces the main characters in the series and shows how individuals can become defined by aspects of their behaviour. The characters are encouraged to examine their self-perceptions and to challenge them. The idea that behaviour can be changed, if the desire to change it exists, is introduced.

Story Two - Deciding to Change
The characters are encouraged to take responsibility for their behaviour, common excuses for avoiding responsibility are examined. Behaviour is discussed in an objective manner and the way behaviours are learned is explored. The need for motivation is stressed in terms of individual reasons for change.

Story Three - The Brain and the Body
This story looks at how the brain controls all behaviours by sending commands to the body. It differentiates between voluntary and involuntary actions and looks, in greater detail, at how we learn. Examples are given of how voluntary orders can become automatic when practised and reinforced. The characters offer aspects of their behaviour that occur automatically, i.e., without having to think about it.

Story Four - Stopping and Thinking

Here strategies for blocking automatic thoughts and actions are discussed. Examples of the ways of overriding the brains commands are given which the reader is encouraged to practise to see that this can be accomplished. The 'stop and think' strategy is introduced, showing how it can be applied. The power of imagination and the role of positive self-talk are examined.

Story Five - Feelings and Beliefs

This story emphasises that when thoughts, feelings and beliefs are in positive congruence then behaviour change is more easily attained. It looks at the context of behaviours, both negative and positive. The reader is encouraged to recognise that behaviour may be a signal for help. The purpose here is to let the reader become aware that there are other means of communicating feelings available that can allow problems to be dealt with in a more constructive and effective way. The role of beliefs in building, or diminishing, self-confidence is examined. Problems are defined in individual and collective 'best interest' terms.

Story Six - Recording and Rewarding

This book shows how self-monitoring, self-recording and self-rewarding can take place. The characters are observed monitoring their behaviour using record books and timers. Rewards, both concrete and internal, are discussed. The impor-tance of practice in mastering these techniques is discussed.

Story Seven - Starting to Change

The characters in the story now apply the techniques they have learned and practised within the framework of a CBT intervention. It demonstrates what the readers themselves will be doing in the following weeks. The main strategies are recapped and potential pitfalls are discussed, showing how these can be effectively overcome when expected and planned for. The reader observes the characters' growing feelings of self-belief and control.

Section 2 - Application: Weeks 8 - 12

When all the stories and activities are completed the pupils commence the second stage of the programme, the applica-tion section. This accounts for weeks 8 - 12 of the pro-gramme. Here the pupils apply their skills through a four week intervention aimed at developing self-control skills in the classroom context with respect, initially, to on task behaviour. This section is designed to allow pupils to practise, and become more skilled in, the self-control techniques they have learned about in the previous lessons. Although the monitoring, recording and rewarding is carried out by the pupil, it is essential that group meetings continue to be carried out on a weekly basis during this period.

Record Books

Each pupil receives a record book on which to register their target behaviours, set their daily targets, note their weekly goals and select their weekly reward. These books are used for self-monitoring and self-evaluation,

Goals

On-task behaviour is usually a component of the weekly target, i.e., sitting in seats, putting up hands to speak and working hard. As the intervention progresses the pupils are encouraged to add other target behaviours, e.g., 'be nice to friends in class' or 'keep my work neat'. These pupil selected behaviours are undertaken when it is felt that the pupil is sufficiently practised in self-control skills to cope with monitoring and recording two behaviours. At this stage the teacher should help the pupil choose a behaviour problem that is related to their life in school and to ensure that this problem is appropriate for the pupil to tackle (i.e. not too complex or requiring too much time for change to occur).

Targets

Targets are set by the pupil on a weekly basis with help from the teacher if necessary. Traditionally they begin small and increase as the pupil's skills develop. There are two aspects to this; firstly lesson targets which are rewarded with a smiley face and secondly weekly targets where pupils can earn a self-selected reward. At the end of each lesson the pupils note whether they have achieved their target and, if so, draw a smiley face on their record books. At the end of each week the pupils add up the number of smiley faces and calculate whether they have achieved their weekly goals. If they have been successful in achieving their weekly goals they can then claim their self-selected reward.

Rewards

Rewards should be guided by the teacher in terms of appropriateness and expense. Rewards are usually concrete and social to begin with becoming more internal as the programme progresses.

Detailed procedures are given in Section 2 of the publication.

References

ASHMAN, A. F. & CONWAY, R. N. F. (1989) Cognitive Strategies for Special Education. Routledge, London.

BECK, A. T. (1963) Thinking and Depression. Archives of General Psychiatry, 9, 324-333.

COOPER, P. & UPTON, G. (1990) Turning Conflict into Co-operation: An Ecosystem Approach to Interpersonal Conflict and its Relevance to Pastoral Care in Schools. Pastoral Care.

DURLAK, J. A., FUHRMAN, T. & LAMPMAN, C. (1991) Effectiveness of Cognitive-Behaviour Therapy for Maladaptive Children: A Meta-Analysis. Psychological Bulletin, 14, 204-214.

DiGUISEPPE, R. (1989) Cognitive Therapy with Children. In A. Freeman, K. M. Simon, L. E. Beutler & H. Arkowitz (eds), Comprehensive Handbook of Cognitive Therapy. Plenum Press, New York.

ELLIS, A. (1962) Reason and Emotion in Psychotherapy. Lyle Stuart, New York.

THE ELTON REPORT (1989) Discipline in Schools. HMSO. London.

FOREHAND, R. & WIERSON, M. (1993) The Role of Developmental Factors in Planning Behavioural Intervention for Children: Disruptive Behaviour as an Example. Behaviour Therapy, 11, 117-141.

KADZIN, (1975) Behaviour Modification in Applied Settings. Dorsey Press, Homewood, Illinois

KENDALL, P.C. (1993) Cognitive-Behavioural Therapies with Youth: Guiding Theory, Current Status and Emerging Developments. Journal of Consulting and Clinical Psychology, 61(2), 235-247.

KENDALL, P. C. & BRASWELL, L. (1985) Cognitive-Behavioural Therapy for Young Children. The Guilford Press, New York.

MEICHENBAUM, D. (1977) Cognitive Behaviour Modification. Plenum Press, New York.

MEICHENBAUM, D. (1979) Teaching Children Self-Control. In B. Lahey & A. Kadzin (eds) Advances in Clinical Child Psychology. Plenum Press, New York.

PIAGET, J. (1950) The Psychology of Intelligence. Trans. M. Percy & D. G. Berlyne. Routledge Keegan Paul, London.

PIAGET, J. (1972) Psychology and Epistemology: Towards a Theory of Knowledge. Trans. P. A. Wells. Penguin Books, London.

POWELL, M. B. & OEI, T. P. S. (1991) Cognitive Processes underlying the Behaviour Change in Cognitive Behaviour Therapy with Childhood Disorders: A Review of Experimental Evidence. Behavioural Psychotherapy, 19, 247-265.

RAE, T. (1998) Dealing with Feeling. Lucky Duck Publishing, Bristol.

RONEN, T. (1991) Intervention Package for Treating Sleep Disorders in a Four Year Old Girl. Behaviour Therapy and Experimental Psychiatry, 22, 141-148.

RONEN, T. (1993) Decision Making about Children's Therapy. Child Psychiatry and Human Development, 23, 259-272.

RONEN, T. (1994) Imparting Self-control in the School Setting. Child and Family Behaviour Therapy, 16, 1-20.

RONEN, T. (1995) From What Kind of Self-Control can Children Benefit? Journal of Cognitive Psychotherapy: An International Quarterly, 9, 45-61.

RONEN, T. (1996) Self-Control Exposure Therapy for Treating Children's Anxieties. Child and Family Behaviour Therapy, 18, 1-17.

RONEN, T. (1997) Cognitive Developmental Therapy With Young Children. Wiley, England.

RONEN, T. & WOZNER, Y. (1995) A Self-Control Intervention Package for the Treatment of Primary Nocturnal Enuresis. Child and Family Behaviour Therapy, 17, 1-20.

RONEN, T., WOZNER, Y. & RAHAV, G. (1992) Cognitive Intervention in Enuresis. Child and Family Behaviour Therapy, 14, 1-20.

ROSENBAUM, M. S. & DRABMAN, R. S. (1979) Self-Control Training in the Classroom: A Review and Critique. Journal of Applied Behaviour Analysis, 12, 467-485.

ROSENBAUM, M. & RONEN, T. (1991) Self-Control and Education for Self-Control: Development of a Rating Scale. Paper Presented at the 25th Anniversary of the Association of Advancement of Behaviour Therapy (AABT), New York.

SHELDON, B. (1995) Cognitive Behavioural Therapy: Research, Practice and Philosophy. Routledge, London.

WHITE, M. (1999) Picture This, Guided Imagery for Circle Time. Lucky Duck Publishing, Bristol.

Section 1

The characters

All the pupils are in the same class: aged 9 - 10 years.

Yusuf
is kind to animals.
He likes to chat in class.

Sam
is helpful to others.
He draws on his desktop
without thinking about it.

Dionne
is eager and enthusiastic.
She talks over other
people's conversations.

Tina
is helpful at home.
She is easily distracted.

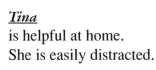

Mrs Wood
is their teacher.
She is good at her job.
She loses her temper easily.

Contents

Teacher Notes for Lesson 1

Aims
- to enable identification with the main characters in the series
- to encourage the distinction between an individual and their behaviour.

Topics for discussion after reading the story

1. The positive and negative points of each character in the booklet:

    Yusuf - Kind to animals but would rather chat than work in class.
    Sam - Helpful to others but draws on desks without thinking.
    Dionne - Eager and enthusiastic but doesn't give others a chance to speak.
    Tina - Likes to help her mum but is very easily distracted.
    Mrs. Wood - A great teacher but loses her temper easily.

2. Choose a familiar character from a class novel or a common reading book. List their positive and negative points.

3. List personal positive and negative points. How do the pupils think other people see them: mum, brother, teacher, friend, neighbour? Is it fair or true to label the pupil in a negative way because of an aspect of the way they act?

Worksheet 1 (Optional)

1. Match the behaviours to the character.

2. Main points to be highlighted:

- Behaviour means the way a person acts.

- Everyone has good and bad aspects of their behaviour. Even teachers!

- Often people focus on the negative character traits of others, ignoring the positive. This is not a true reflection of the individual.

- If the worst is expected of someone often they will deliver and often they will begin to expect it of themselves.

- Behaviour can be taught, just like any other subject.

Book 1
Looking at Behaviour

This is Sam. Sam is a friendly nine-year old boy. I'm sure you'd like him if you ever met him. He's got red spiky hair and lots of freckles. He likes football, pizza and he drinks Shake-a-Mite which is a special drink that he thinks makes him much, much better at football, (actually the drink itself doesn't work but don't tell him that!). Sam lives at home with his parents, his big sister Janine and everyone's special baby, Sammyboy the pup.

Sam

Sam, of course, goes to school and he has three very special friends there; Dionne, who plays football with him, and is almost as good as he is, Yusuf, who lives nearby and helps him to look after Sammyboy, and Tina who keeps them all entertained by telling wonderful stories.

Dionne

Tina

Yusuf

Their teacher is called Mrs. Wood. Everyone thinks they're very lucky being in Mrs. Wood's class because a few years ago she was voted Champion Teacher of the Year by a local paper. Everyone knew about it because one day the school was covered in balloons. The TV cameras were there and the Mayor made a speech. Mrs. Wood was very happy that day.

Mrs Wood

Like nearly every other boy and girl in the country there are some things the children like about school and some things they don't. At the same time there are some things about the children that Mrs. Wood likes and some things she just doesn't.....

She likes it when Sam sharpens her pencils......

but not when he uses them to draw on the desks.....

She likes it that Dionne's so keen to tell her things.....

but not when she shouts everyone else down and doesn't give them a chance to speak.......

or when Tina sees something interesting going on
out of the window and gets out of her seat to have
a look.....

or when Yusuf starts to play "hide Sally's crayons"
when he should be working.

No, Mrs. Wood does not like it one little bit. And once or twice, when
her little twins have kept her up all the night before, or the car hasn't
started or the caretaker has accidently put the day's worksheets in
the bin, it has made her very, very cross indeed.

Her eyebrows go down, her shoulders rise up almost to her ears, her
skin goes pale and she starts to tremble.

The rest of the class grow silent except for the group who haven't yet noticed and then a terrifying voice explodes......

"SAM, DIONNE, YUSUF, TINA!
WILL YOU PLEASE JUST STOP!!"

At times like this things aren't very good between
the children and Mrs. Wood.

They think, "Why is she shouting at me?"
She thinks, "Why did they do that?"

Then they think, "She must think we're no good."
Then she thinks, "They mustn't care about school."

Then they think, "Why is she ALWAYS picking on us like this?"
Then she thinks, "Why do they NEVER do what I want them to do?"

Unfortunately this has been going on for a while now and the children are
not feeling very good about school at all.

Sam's beginning to think that he's no good at anything, that he's always getting picked on and he can't help it. Sam's sister thinks Mrs. Wood is right. "You're nothing but trouble," she shouts at him.

Dionne's parents have been called up to school and they're cross with her too.

"Why don't you just behave?" they say.
"Why won't you just be good?"

"You're such a nuisance Dionne," says her mother.
"You're letting us all down."

Tina's starting to believe that she's always got her head in the clouds, while Yusuf thinks he's just a chatterbox.

Even some of their other school friends are starting to avoid them. "Don't sit next to them," they whisper. "They'll just get you into trouble."

Poor children. They're not feeling good about themselves at all.

They begin to think that school is awful, their teacher is horrible, they have no other friends, they upset their parents, they're hopeless at everything. Well, since they've got such a reputation they figure that they might as well just stay in their gang and be what everyone expects them to be....... BAD.

But wait, aren't they forgetting some things?

Like how kind Yusuf is to
Sammyboy the pup?

And how Tina's so
keen to help clean
the house?

And how Sam's a lightning soccer shooter when he has his Shake-A-Mite.

And how Dionne's the only one in the class who will dive into the rubbish bin to find Mrs. Wood's lost worksheets.

Are the children really bad ..... or is it just that some of the ways they act aren't so good?

Mrs. Wood, who by now has had a full week of unbroken sleep, a newly serviced car and a secure cupboard full of worksheets, thinks about this.

No, she thinks, Sam, Yusuf, Tina and Dionne are actually very nice children who, deep down, she's very fond of.

For goodness sake, thinks Mrs. Wood as she sips her herbal tea. If they had trouble learning how to read or write I wouldn't be shouting at them, I'd be teaching them! It's all about how they act and, if they've learned to do lots of different things like ride a bike, and their seven times tables, why can't they learn new ways to act.

"Well," says Mrs. Wood, speaking to no-one in particular. "They will!"

And who better to teach them than ... **Champion Teacher of the Year!**

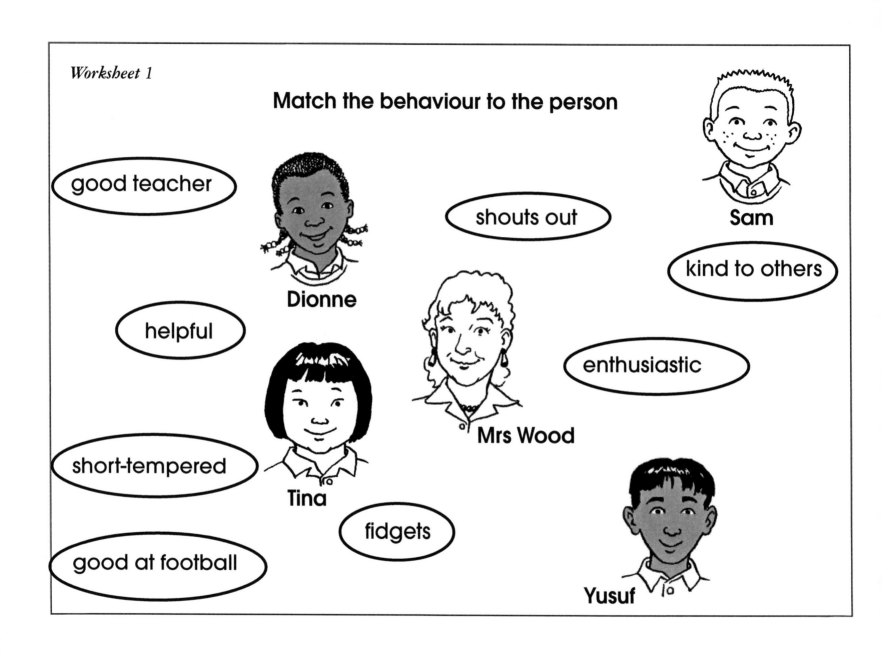

Teacher Notes for Lesson Two

Aims

- to show how false beliefs can be challenged
- to explain the nature of learning
- to show the importance of having personal reasons to change.

Topics for discussions after reading the story

1. Who is responsible for our behaviour?

   Examine Sam's excuses for not taking responsibility for his actions.

   What do people say when they're not taking responsibility?

   For example:

   It's not my fault.

   He/she made me do it.

   You're always picking on me.

2. What type of things do we say about ourselves?

   List both positive and negative self-statements.

   Examine the truth of negative statements by relating them to the evidence.

   For example:

Statement	Challenge
I can't learn that.	What have I learnt to do well?
I'm no good.	What are my good points?
Everyone's against me.	Who supports me?

3. Discuss common examples of learning new skills and examine whether the children experienced the stages of learning, ie, being conscious of commanding the body in certain ways until the process became automatic. For example learning to ride a bike, using the computer, learning a dance routine.

4. Discuss the reasons Sam had for wanting to change. What individual things do the pupils want to stop doing and why?
        For example:

Behaviour to change	_Reasons_
Stop talking in class.	To learn more.
	So I won't be shouted at.
	So everyone else can learn.

Worksheet 2 (Optional)

True or False - Questions about taking responsibility.

Main points to be highlighted

- As the individual has control over their minds and bodies, their behaviour is within their control even though they may not realise it.

- Just because a person believes something about themselves doesn't mean it's accurate. Negative beliefs should be examined to see if they're true.

- Learning new behaviours is difficult to begin with but with practice it becomes easy.

- As change isn't easy it's important that the individual has their own reasons to change. This will help them during the difficult stage of transition.

Book 2
Deciding to Change

Mrs. Wood keeps the group in at lunch one day to have a chat with them.

"I want to talk to you about your behaviour, about the way you've been acting in class," she says in her nicest, sweetest, 'you can talk to me I'm your friend' sort-of voice.

Sam looks at her grumpily and says "You're always picking on us. It's just not fair. I can't speak for the others but I can't help it you know. I try to be good and then something makes me do those things. It's just not my fault."

Mrs. Wood smiles and nods patiently. "I understand how you're feeling Sam. But, you know, I'm really not meaning to pick on you. It just annoys me that you're not following our rules and I suppose what I'm doing is telling you each time you break them." She sighs. "I know that all this shouting isn't working though, and it seems to be making everything worse so I think we should just change tack."

"I'd like to try something new with you, if you don't mind, I'd like to teach you about self-control, about how *you* can control your behaviour."

Yusuf isn't sure what's got into Mrs. Wood and he doesn't really know what she's talking about. Only yesterday she was yelling at them and now she's being all friendly.

"The first and most important thing you have to realise," she continues, "is that your behaviour is all up to you. You might *think* that other people make you do things and you might *feel* that you can't help what you do. But the bottom line is that it is *always* up to you."

"Who owns your body Dionne?" she asks.

Dionne hasn't thought about this one before.
"Umm, my mum I suppose," she says hopefully.

Mrs. Wood shakes her head, "Try again."

"Umm. Me?"

"YES! And who owns your mind?"

"Me!" shouts Tina.

"And the way you act....and the things you do ....and your behaviour?"

"We do!" the children reply.

Mrs. Wood nods and smiles. "Yes children, you own them all but you don't know how to use them in the best way for you. It's like being given a roomful of toys and not knowing how to play with them."

Yusuf sighs, "But how I am I going to learn how to change. It's no good! I'm hopeless, I can't learn anything."

"That's your feelings talking, Yusuf," says Mrs. Wood
"Let's look at what you are saying and see if it's true.
Now you *say* that you can't learn anything, but look at
all the things you have learned already - like how to
read and write. Think of one of the first things you
learned - walking."

"First you could only crawl and
then you wanted to walk."

"I want to walk?"

"Like all babies you would first get up on your feet. Then you would walk holding on to furniture, and then you would try to walk on your own."

"Why did I bother?"

"But you fell down didn't you? I'm sure you fell down lots and lots of times. Perhaps you even thought to yourself that it was easier just to stay crawling."

"But you didn't. You kept at it until you walked easily - you practised and practised until you got it right."

"Can anyone think of anything else they've learned to do well?"

Sam thinks for a moment. "Yes. It's a bit like when I was learning to ride my bike. I remember how hard it was. I had all these things to remember, like looking ahead, keeping my balance, moving the pedals around with my feet and turning the handlebars in the direction I wanted to go. I kept on and on falling off."

"I remember thinking that it would be much easier if I could just keep my stabilisers on for ever! But I wanted to be able to ride properly so I just kept on and then one day it all came together."

"And now?" asks Mrs. Wood.

Sam smiles as he thinks of himself dashing about on his bike in the park doing skids and wheelies without a second thought.

Sam gives a shrug, "Not bad I suppose..."

"So you see," says Mrs. Wood, "You *can* learn things and we're only talking about a few of the things you've learned to do - there are lots more. What you were saying about yourselves wasn't true."

"I suppose so."

"Not only that. You've learned lots of difficult things. It took a lot of effort and thought to begin with but in the end, after lots of practice, you could do them easily. Like riding your bike, in the end you could do it without having to think about it at all!"

"But," Mrs. Wood goes on, "There's one more important thing to remember about learning something new. You really have to want to do it because that's what will help you to keep going when the learning gets hard and mistakes keep happening. You have to have your own reasons for changing."

She looks straight at the children and smiles.

"So, do you want to learn how to act differently?" she pauses for a moment.

"I'm going to let you think about it. If you want to I'll see you here same time next week."

The children sit for a while and talk - Would it be worth the effort to learn all these new things? Even if what Mrs. Wood said was true, that they could learn how to control themselves, what good would it do them?

Sam thinks about when he had learned to ride his bike - he kept at it because he was not going to be the only one of his friends still using stabilisers and also because he really wanted to be the best. What good would it do him? Well, for one thing he'd get some peace - he was getting tired of being shouted at by Mrs. Wood, his mum and dad, and even Janine was getting at him.

Tina thinks of how proud her mum would be if she would do better at school. Dionne wonders, if she wasn't getting into trouble at school and being kept in at lunchtime, would she be picked for the football team because she could practise more.

Yusuf knows that he's tired of feeling different to the others in the class because he is the one who seems to be getting into trouble most. He likes people knowing who he is but it would be nice to be known for a reason other than that.

"You want to try?" asks Dionne looking at the others.

"I'd give it a go," says Tina. "And you two?"

"Yeah, I'm in," replies Yusuf.

Sam nods and grins, "Me too."

And with that the children put their hands together in the centre of the table and make their pact.

True or False?

Teacher Notes for Lesson 3

Aims

This lesson will explain that:
- behaviour is connected to learning and practising
- the brain controls all actions
- some thoughts are automatic
- automatic thoughts can be changed.

Topics for discussion after reading the story

1. Ask the pupils for examples of actions that they have voluntary control over;
    for example, reading, writing, moving limbs,
  and things the brain has total control of;
    for example, breathing and heart rate.

2. Ask the children for their experiences of learning new skills.
  Say, for example, playing an instrument or using roller-skates or a skateboard.
  How do they compare to someone who is well practised in these skills?
  Do these relate to Sam's experience of learning to ride a bike?
  Can they identify with the different stages involved?
    for example roller-skating:
      moving around slowly holding on to people and objects
      moving around more confidently by oneself
      skating quickly from one place to another.

3. Ask the children for examples of automatic actions (things that they do without thinking) that occur in class. E.g., shouting out, fidgeting and fiddling, day dreaming, getting out of the seat or talking to others.

Worksheet 3 (optional)

1. Identifying the main stages in learning to ride a bicycle - adding text to accompany illustrations.

2. Main points to be highlighted:

- the brain controls all actions through commanding the body
- the ones that we can exert control over are learned through practice
- learning and practising will help establish new behaviours and make them become automatic
- as automatic behaviours are learned they can be intercepted to allow other behaviour to become automatic.

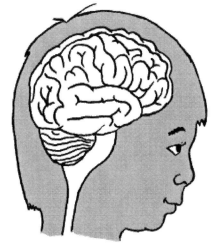

Book 3
The Brain & the Body

The next week Mrs. Wood is delighted see the group waiting for her.

     "Great to see you," she says and gives them a quick hug.

     "Before you learn about self-control it's useful to find out about the brain and how it works. That way you can learn to use it to help you."

Mrs. Wood points at Tina's head.

     "Inside your head, sitting safely within your skull, is your brain."

She takes out a picture.

"This is a picture of how it looks. It's a very clever thing. It is the body's control centre and it sends messages to all the different parts of the body and messages get sent back to it."

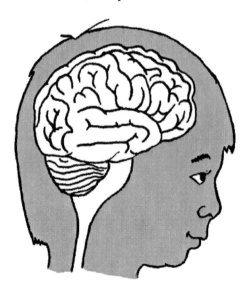

She points at the library shelf and continues.

"Piles of big, heavy books have been written about what the brain does. Even if you spent all your time learning about it you probably still wouldn't know everything it does, it's so complicated. So we'll just think about it in simple terms."

MR BRAIN THE BOSS

"The brain controls everything that the body does - I think of it as a big boss watching over the whole body all the time, even when you're asleep."

"Like a very hardworking boss of a factory," says Sam, "I can picture him in my head."

"It could be a woman you know,"
Dionne points out.

"That's right Dionne," says Mrs. Wood,
"But it doesn't really matter. You think of
it the way that suits you."

"Does the boss have lots of workers?"
Yusuf wonders aloud.

MS BRAIN THE BOSS

"Oh, lots and lots of workers," replies Mrs. Wood. "And all the workers
have different jobs. Some workers make the heart beat or the lungs
take in air. Some might move the muscles in your legs to make you
run, or move your tongue and lips to make you speak."

"Some workers just take messages back and forth from the brain to different parts of the body. Think of them running down the body's pathways with little messages like 'beat the heart' or 'bend that knee.'"

"And of course messages get brought back to the brain. Think of this. You're hungry and you find some ham or something at the back of the fridge. You're about to bite into it when you take a sniff and stop. What has happened is that a message has been delivered to the brain telling it about the food's smell. The brain thinks that it might be bad and harmful to eat so you don't."

"Anyway the brain is always giving the body orders, sending messages to do all those things we've just talked about and many, many more."

"Some things the brain will do and keep doing whether you want it to or not, like breathing, and keeping your heart beating - you do these things without having to think about it and you won't be able to stop doing them just by trying. In these cases your brain is in control because it wants you to survive."

"But in other cases you can control what the brain tells your body to do because .... the brain may be the boss of the factory but you are the owner!"

"Let's look at what happens when you learn something new. We'll look at riding a bike seeing as we've talked about it before."

"You want to learn so you give your brain lots of little instructions."

"The brain commands your body to carry out these instructions by sending messages to the different parts of your body."

"After a while the brain gets the picture of what it means to ride a bike and knows exactly how to command the body, so, instead of having to remember all those little instructions, you can do it without even thinking about it. All you need do is want to do it, get on your bike, and away you go!"

"Something that started out hard is now very, very easy to do. The brain is giving the orders and carrying them out *automatically* and you're free to think of other things. What other things have you learned to do automatically?" asks Mrs. Wood.

Tina thinks...... "I know, learning to use my computer. I don't have to think of all those little instructions any more."

"That's a good one!" laughs Mrs. Wood. "I'd say the best example for me would be learning how to drive - you'll realise all about it when you learn. But I was thinking of other things for you. You know those things you say you do in class without thinking Dionne?"

"Like talking and not working during lessons you mean?" she replies.

"Yes. And Sam, what about walking about during class and fidgeting with things? And Yusuf, what about you carrying on with the other children?" Mrs. Wood continues.

The group look surprised.

"Are these things that we have learned to do automatically as well?" asks Tina.

"Exactly!" Mrs. Wood claps her hands. "Somehow you learned to do these things and the truth is you can unlearn them."

"Next week I'll tell you all about blocking automatic thoughts and replacing them with new ones."

What is this child thinking?

Teacher Notes for Lesson 4

Aims

- to show that automatic thoughts can be changed with the help of stopping and thinking techniques, imagining and self-talk.

Activity

Practise stopping the brain's commands using Sam's examples - running on the spot, holding the arms above the head, etc. Try others that the children volunteer.

Topics for discussion after reading the story

1. Ask each pupil for an example of their own behaviour. Could they use the stopping and thinking technique to help them? What would they imagine?

    For example:

        shouting out - Realise——— Stop——Imagine sitting quietly, listening or working.

        getting out of seat - Realise———Freeze———Imagine sitting in your seat.

2. What self-statements could the pupils use to encourage themselves?

    For example:

        shouting out - I want to be quiet so I, the rest of the class can learn. I can do it if I try.

        getting out of seat - I want to stay in my seat so I can do my work.

**Worksheet 4 (Optional)**

Traffic light worksheet adapted from an activity in 'Dealing with Feeling' by Tina Rae 1998 (available from Lucky Duck Publishing).

**Main points to be highlighted**

- once we become aware that we are following the brain's commands we can stop them
- stopping what you are doing and thinking about the way you want to act helps
- saying encouraging things to yourself helps.

Book 4
Stopping and Thinking

"This week," says Mrs. Wood, "I want to show you how you can block or ignore the brain's commands."

Mrs. Wood raises her arms. "Try this - hold your hands over your head. In a while they'll start to feel tired and sore. That's the brain telling you to relax them."

The children hold their hands over their heads. After a while Tina starts to moan and Yusuf says that it's sore.

"You can choose to ignore that command and keep them up a little bit longer. Don't keep them up too long or it will really hurt!" says Mrs. Wood, laughing.

After a minute the arms all flop down by the children's sides.

"There you are!" says Mrs. Wood. "That's an example of how you can block a command from the brain."

"Another thing you could do is to try running on the spot for a while. See if you can tell when the brain is commanding you to stop."

Dionne jumps up and begins to run. She runs quite quickly but then begins to tire.

"See if you can keep going a little longer."

"I'm trying Mrs. Wood, really I am, but I think my brain is yelling at me to stop!" pants Dionne.

"Well done Dionne." Mrs. Wood looks pleased. "You can sit down now. What you're doing is stopping the brain's commands!"

"You see, you can control your actions if you concentrate. In both these cases though, it's not a good idea to block these types of thoughts because they are all about keeping the body well - and anyway you'd have to do what the brain wants in the end as you'd be too exhausted to keep going."

"But there are other commands that you can block without doing you any harm. I'm thinking of those things you have learned to do automatically. The thing is there's a special way to do it."

"Remember you are the owner of your brain and in these cases you can tell it what to do."

"Let's say you're in a lesson where you should be working by yourself. If you realise you're doing something you shouldn't you should say to your-self STOP. Can you imagine a great big stop sign, like the one you see on the road?"

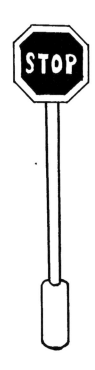

"Picture that."

"There are other ways to imagine this. You have to choose the one that suits you."

"You could imagine standing in front of one of those brain messengers we talked about earlier and holding up your hand and shouting STOP."

"Or I could imagine a red traffic light," says Sam.

"Yes. Whichever is the most powerful picture for you,"

"Once you've stopped you then have to THINK."

"What do we think about?" asks Yusuf.

"What you want to be doing. Like sitting in your seat, or working hard. Imagine this in your mind now, make a nice bright picture of one of the ways you want to act."

"You can also say things to yourself that will help you. Like 'I know I can change,' or 'this is hard at the moment but I'll get better with practice'."

"These things will help your brain carry out the order you give it."

"We'll be practising them in the next few weeks."

Traffic Light Control

Stop!   ......and calm down.

1. What is the problem?

Wait

2. What is the feeling?

3. List some possible solutions.

1

Go

2

4. Make a plan.

3

Teacher Notes for Lesson 5

Aims

- to show the role of feelings and beliefs in influencing behaviour.

Topics for discussion after reading the story

1. Ask the children for examples of negative and positive influences on behaviour.
   For example:
   > Negative - A bad fight at home, being bullied, failing an exam, missing a goal, a pet dying.
   > Positive - A birthday, winning a prize, making a new friend.

2. Discuss the steps a child should take if something is really bothering them:
   - talk to someone who can be trusted - a teacher, parent, friend or relative
   - ring a child helpline.

Activity

Ask the children to dream that they're being good at something they want to succeed in.
   Ask detailed questions about the picture, for example, for sitting working hard at their desks, ask:-
   - What, exactly, are they doing in their picture?
   - Is the image colour or black and white?
   - Are they watching themselves or are they in the picture?
   - What clothes are they wearing?
   - Can they smell the classroom - chalk dust, wood, etc?

- Are they aware of any sounds? for example: children playing outside, people talking in the corridor, etc.
- Can they feel the wood of the desk, the pencil in their hand?

The purpose here is to create as vivid a picture as possible. Once the children can visualise success, ask how it makes them feel - proud, capable, in control.

(A useful resource to encourage visualisation is "Picture This", an audio-tape with teacher notes written by Murray White, 1999 available from Lucky Duck Publishing.)

Worksheet 5 (optional)

The pupil draws a picture of a way s/he wants to act.

Main points to be highlighted

- Negative and positive feelings can affect behaviour making it better or worse.
- Acting in negative ways can be a way of communicating negative feelings. It is often more effective to deal with a problem by sharing it with someone who can be trusted then, perhaps, the problem can be solved.
- Time and effort will facilitate change but self-belief is just as important.
- Imagining can create a powerful, motivating picture which helps the individual feel that they can achieve what they want.

Book 5
Feelings and Beliefs

"This week," begins Mrs. Wood, "I want to tell you how important our feelings and beliefs are in affecting the way we act."

"How you feel really matters" Mrs. Wood continues. "Do you ever notice that some days I'll be much more cross than others?"

"Yes," says Sam, rolling his eyes, who knows only too well.

The rest of the children start to laugh.

Mrs. Wood gives a stern look. "You know I sometimes think you children expect me to be superhuman. What usually happens is that maybe one of the children has been sick or maybe I've had to spend a lot of time marking and I can't go to my exercise class. Then the next day I'll have a shorter temper than usual. I might get more impatient with a pupil on those days and shout."

"O.K." she continues, "It's not an excuse but it is understandable".

"I understand," says Tina, "My baby sister sometimes keeps us awake all night."

"Thanks Tina" she smiles, "Can anyone else think of any times they've felt like that?"

"I think so," Sam replies. "When my puppy Sammyboy was at the vet for an operation I was worried and everyone at home annoyed me more than usual. I didn't notice at the time. When Sammyboy came back well again I realised how horrible I'd been to them all."

Mrs. Wood nods. "Perhaps if you'd talked about how you felt you wouldn't have acted so badly. The way we act is a message to let other people know how unhappy or angry or confused we feel."

Dionne nods. "There was this girl in my class last year who used to get picked on by a big girl on the way home from school. She had to give her sweets and money and listen to the big girl calling her names. Well, this girl got really mad at what was happening to her so she started to act badly, shouting at the other children and hitting them. The teacher tried lots of ways to get her to stop, like keeping her in at lunch times and bringing her parents up to school. It was only when she told me what was happening to her that she changed. I told her to tell her mum and the teacher. They were able to stop the bullying. When she wasn't angry any more she stopped behaving badly at school."

"Thanks Dionne," says Mrs. Wood, "That's a very good example. So you see, if something is really bothering you it is so important to talk to someone you trust. When something bad is happening to you then that thing should be sorted out first and then you can change the way you act."

"Is anything worrying or bothering you at the moment, besides your problems in school?" Mrs. Wood asks.

"No," say the children except for Tina who is thinking. "I suppose when I haven't had much sleep it affects the way I am in school."

"I'm sure it does Tina," says Dionne. "How about asking your mum to get you some earplugs? That might help."

"Good thinking Dionne!" says Mrs. Wood with a smile. "Anyway Tina, be sure and let me know if it happens again and we'll sort something out. As I said before, it's not an excuse for acting badly but if I know what's bothering you then I can try to find a way of helping you get what you need. Maybe a short rest would do the trick."

Mrs. Wood continues, "When you're feeling bad it can affect the way you act but so can feeling good, in another way of course."

"That time I won the special prize for being the champion teacher, that made me really happy and I got on very well with all my pupils for the rest of that term. Everything seemed to go smoothly but the reality was that I was probably acting much more pleasantly to everyone. Because I believed I was good everyone else seemed to believe it too."

Sam thinks for a moment. "I know when I scored the goal that won the cup for my team I was very happy. For a while after that I didn't seem to do anything wrong and nobody shouted at me. The goal happened because I'd taken my Shake-A-Mite. That's why I always take it before a match."

Mrs. Wood laughs, "I always wondered why you were drinking that disgusting stuff."

"You know Sam," she goes on. "That's a good example of how to use thoughts and feelings and beliefs to help you."

"Let me tell you a secret. It's not that the Shake-A-Mite actually makes you better at football. The fact is that it's because you believe it does, that makes you good."

"What happens before you have a match Sam?" Mrs. Wood asks.
"Do you take it then?"
"Yes."

"And what do you think of?"

"I think of myself as being very strong and very fast and scoring goals."

"And how do you feel?"

"Brilliant, like I'm a fantastic player."

"What has happened here Sam," says Mrs.Wood, "is that you imagine yourself doing well and because you believe you can do it you are super-confident. These things help you to play well, not the Shake-A-Mite."

"Let's think about the things I wanted you to imagine earlier on, the picture of you sitting at your desk working. Now, Yusuf, if you were doing that all the time what would I be saying about you."

"That I'm doing really well."

"Correct!" Mrs. Wood laughs and ruffles Yusuf's hair. "Can you imagine me saying that to you? Can you imagine me telling your parents about how well you were doing? How would I be looking? What would I be saying? Picture it."

"Now picture your parents' faces when I was telling them that and imagine what they'd say. Got the picture?"

"Now tell me how that makes you feel."

Yusuf laughs, "Brilliant really proud."

"Good, that's what I want you to feel when you think of the person you want to be. I want you to feel that you can do it and when you do it will be great."

"Can you believe that children?" Mrs. Wood asks.

"Yes!" says Tina, " I'm definitely beginning to."

Teacher Notes for Lesson 6

Aims
- to consider what makes good rules and why they should be kept
- to consider what behaviour problems are
- to show that reinforcement can help to change automatic behaviour.

Topics for discussion after reading story

1. Discuss some class and school rules. Write on a chart. For each discuss why we should keep them, what would happen if we didn't, what would be the long-term effect and whether ultimately they are of benefit to ourselves and others.

For example:

Rule	Outcome if it isn't kept	Is this desirable?
Put your hand up to speak.	Lots of talking. No one can hear lessons. Difficulty concentrating.	No.

2. Discuss the group's behaviour problems.
- Sam - fidgeting and fiddling - not paying attention - won't learn.
- Yusuf - talking - not paying attention- keeping himself and others back.
- Dionne - shouting out - can't listen to others' views - annoys other children.
- Tina - daydreaming - not concentrating - won't learn.

Expand the discussion to include some examples of the pupils' behaviours in class and discuss how these might be problems.

3. Discuss the different types of reinforcement - symbolic and social. (Symbolic rewards should always be small).

Symbolic	_Social_
Yo-yo	Teacher saying "Well done"
Fancy hair clip	A round of applause
Diary	A handshake
Bouncy ball	A hug from someone you love
Badge	Praise
Certificate	Cheers from classsmates.

Activity Worksheet 6

Practise the monitoring of a behaviour using the record sheet.

Target behaviour: Working hard. (Explain and agree the meaning of "working hard".)

Set a mechanical timer to go off five times at random intervals during a ten minute period while the children complete some simple work (This means resetting it each time it rings). Keep the timer out of sight so that the children don't know when, exactly, the bell will ring. At each ring of the bell the children should look at themselves to see what they're doing. If their behaviour is on target at that point in time (don't consider any other target other than the one specified) they can give themselves a tick on the record sheet. At the end of the period the children should count up all their ticks.

Main points to be highlighted

- Rules should exist for the benefit of the individual and the group.
- In order to engage a pupil's motivation they should have some individual sense of why their behaviour is a problem.
- Changing automatic thoughts can be difficult because we are usually unaware of them. It is only when the pupil starts to practise self-monitoring then they begin to develop an awareness of when they are happening.
- Stress the importance of feeling pleased with personal achievements and how that is a reward in itself.

Book 6
Recording & Rewarding

Mrs. Wood begins, "We were talking a few weeks ago about how to stop the brain's commands by using thoughts, do you remember?"

"Yes, you mean stopping and thinking?" asks Tina.

"Exactly! Well, this week we're going to practise it with the ways you act. What things should we look at?"

"All the bad stuff I do in school," says Sam.

"Good idea. First of all let's think about what is a problem for one person won't be a problem for another."

"Look at me, I bite my nails.." Mrs. Wood holds out her hands. "I see that your bite you nails too Yusuf."

"Yeah," says Yusuf looking at his hands . "But I don't mind."

"So nail biting is a problem for me but it's not a problem for you. That's because problems, like reasons to change, are up to the person."

"Nail biting is a problem for me because I'd like lovely long red nails. But it isn't to you because it doesn't matter to you."

"Too right," thinks Yusuf.

The others giggle thinking of Yusuf with long, red nails.

"Let's go over all the school behaviours that are a problem to you" Mrs. Wood continues. "OK. Let's see. There's walking around the class...um...shouting out, and..."

"...And talking to the others and not working," Yusuf adds shuffling his feet.

"Now Yusuf, why are these a problem to you?"

"Because I'm breaking the class rules and I get shouted at."

"Yes, that's true, but there's more. Good rules are there to help you and everyone else in the class. Think about the rule that says that you should work quietly. Why do we have that rule? Because it would be hard to get work done if everyone was talking. The real problem then is that if you're noisy when you should be working you are not just breaking a rule, you are keeping yourself and others from learning."

"I see," Yusuf nods.

"Why do we have the rule about walking in the corridor do you think?"

"If everyone ran there would be accidents," says Sam.

"So this rule was made to keep everyone safe .... What I'm saying is don't think of these things just as rules. Think about how it affects you personally and then you might be more keen to change it. Does that make sense?"

The children nod thoughtfully.

Target

How many times will the timer ring?

Put your ticks here

How did you score?

"Anyway back to changing the way you act," Mrs. Wood continues. "The first thing you do is become more aware of when the actions you want to change are happening. Let's choose just one of those behaviours we talked about earlier."

"We'll choose something that's not too difficult to begin with... like.... not working."

"To start you need to get a record sheet to help you become more aware."

"During some lessons I'm going to ask you to make a note of if you are working when you hear this bell."

Mrs. Wood rings the bell on the kitchen timer.

"To begin with I'll set it to go off about ten times each lesson and I'll choose a couple of lessons to do this each day for the week."

"So," says Tina, "the bell will go off lots and lots of times each lesson."

"Yes Tina," says Mrs. Wood, "It goes off at different times sometimes only one minute after the last one and sometimes you might have to wait five minutes or more. Believe me it's better this way. It means you won't get to know when it will go off."

"Let's have a practice now, just for ten minutes."

Mrs. Wood gives each child a record sheet and a rough work jotter. They fill in their targets on the record sheet. Then Mrs. Wood asks them to write down why they want to change how they act in school. As the children are working she sets the timer to go off 5 times. When the children hear the bell they stop and think about what they're doing and draw a tick if they've been working. At the end of the ten minutes they look at their record sheets.

Target

I will work hard

How many times will the timer ring?   5

Put your ticks here

✓ ✓ ✓ ✓ ✓

How did you score?

$\frac{5}{5}$

"I was working each time the bell went! I can do it!" shouts Dionne excitedly.

"Me too!" shout the others.

"Good for you!" claps Mrs. Wood. "Now you can see how well you've done."

"You'll be doing this in class soon but first there are other things I can tell you about that will help you, like rewards. Rewards are nice and they help you to change your behaviour."

"What do mean by rewards?" Dionne asks.

"Well, it's up to each person what works as a reward. It has to be something that you'd like. Nothing very special or expensive but something that would make you feel good."

"Let's look at some. Some people like balloons or sweets. One girl I know chose a yo-yo while another little boy chose a diary. Can you think of any more you'd like?"

"I'd like a lolly!" says Tina.

"A comb for my hair!" adds Dionne.

Sam thinks, "Could I get a tin of food for Sammyboy?" he asks.

"Yes!" says Mrs. Wood "No problem!"

"Other things that might work as rewards for you are certificates."

CERTIFICATE

_____

_____

of excellence

"Now what about you, Yusuf? You haven't told us what you'd like as a reward."

Yusuf smiles shyly and says, "This sounds silly but I'd like to stay in at break with you some day and have a chat."

Mrs. Wood laughs. "That's so you!" she says ruffling his hair. "I'm glad you said that because it shows that rewards don't have to be things. Some people prefer notes from the teacher, or their parents or classmates about how pleased they are with them. Then they can put it up on the bedroom wall."

"But it's just as important that you learn to become pleased with yourself. One way of doing this would be to start writing things about yourself and read them out to the class."

Tina looks at Mrs. Wood. "I think I'd feel embarrassed."

"That's OK," she replies. "The important thing to realise is that in the end the reward should simply be knowing that you can control yourself and that you can make your brain and body work in the way that's best for you."

"Now I think you know everything that you need to. Remember the three things you have to do:
* Be aware of how you're acting,
* Record it
* Reward it."
"Things might not get better immediately but if you...."

"Practise!" they shout.

"Yes, if you practise you'll soon get the hang of it."

Working on a target

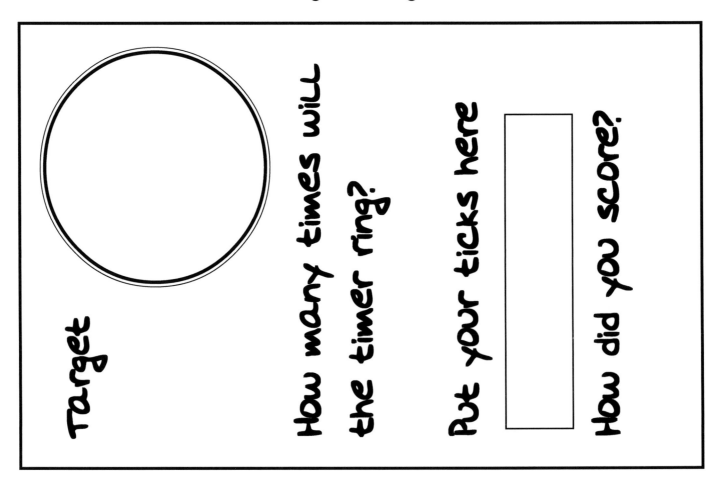

Target

How many times will the timer ring?

Put your ticks here

How did you score?

Teacher Notes for Lesson 7

<u>*Aims*</u>

- To introduce pupils to the procedure for choosing a target behaviour for a given period, monitoring it and rewarding it.
- To show how the techniques of imagining, stopping and thinking, and positive self-talk can be used in helping to achieve goals.
- To illustrate that mistakes are to be expected.

<u>*Topics for discussion after reading the story*</u>

1. Recap on the techniques that can help when changing behaviour, the steps are:

   Beforehand - Decide on the <u>*personal reasons for change*</u>.

   Each morning and other times during the day, <u>*Imagine*</u> the way you want to act, picture yourself doing it.

   <u>*Monitor*</u> your behaviour during the school day.

   Use the <u>*stop and think*</u> technique to change your behaviour if you're not acting the way you want to.

   <u>*Record*</u> the number of times you were on target.

   <u>*Reward*</u> success.

   Stress that the more these techniques are <u>*practised*</u> the more effective they will become.

2. How does Mrs. Wood encourage Yusuf and Tina when they haven't got their smiley faces for the day?

   Can the children think of any other words of encouragement?

3. Explain to the pupils that next week they will be embarking on the programme in class just like the characters in the story.

Main points to be highlighted

- Check that each pupil understands the skills that they will have to use.
- The techniques of stopping and thinking, imagining, self-monitoring, self- recording and self-rewarding will, when practised with behaviours the individual wishes to change, will facilitate a change in behaviour.
- Problems and mistakes are to be expected when learning new ways to act. Change is a slow and sometimes a hard process but can be achieved.

Book 7
Starting to Change

The children rush into the classroom. They are excited because this is the week that they'll be making their self-control plan.

Mrs. Wood brings in their record book- lets, they're called 'My Goal Book'.

She turns to the first page. Step 1.

"OK. There are several things you could change but we'll only start with one. Try to make it a thing that wouldn't be too hard for you all to change. What about working hard during lessons?"

The children fill in their goal for the week in their best writing.

I will work hard during Lessons

"Next you have to choose how many ticks will give you a smiley face token for each session."

How many ✓ for a 🙂 ___ ?

"The bell will go off 10 times each lesson, right?" asks Tina. "So I suppose 10 ticks for each token."

"Oh no Tina! For one thing you're just learning, so start off low and work higher as the weeks go by. Anyway, we never expect anyone to be perfect all the time, everybody has an off day."

"Why don't you start off with 5 times a lesson."

How many ✓ for a  _S_

"Now we will be doing this in two lessons every day. That's two chances to get a token each day and 10 chances each week. How many tokens will you need at the end of week to get your reward?"

"Six? To begin with," suggests Sam.

How many  **for a reward.** **6**

"Yes, I think you could manage that. What do you want to choose for your first reward?"

Sam fills in -   A tin of dog food.

Tina fills in -   A lolly.

Yusuf fills in -   A chat with Mrs. Wood.

Dionne fills in - A comb.

"OK. Good choices everyone" says Mrs. Wood.

"Let's look at the record sheet. Are you clear about filling it in? Explain it to me."

Dionne points to the first box. "Say it's the first lesson on Monday. I put a tick in the box each time the bell rings. At the end of the lesson I count up all my ticks."

"If I have five or more ticks I can draw a smiley face in the bottom box like this" adds Sam.

	Monday	Tuesday	Wednesday	Thursday	Friday
Lesson 1	✓✓✓✓✓✓✓✓				
Lesson 2	✓✓✓✓	✓✓✓✓✓			
Success	😊	😊 😊			
Did you get your goal this week?					

Yusuf continues, "I do the same thing for each of my lessons and at the end of the week if I have enough Smiley face tokens I'll get my reward which is spending my break time with you."

"Great" says Mrs. Wood, "What will you do if you find yourself starting to dream and not working?"

"Simple" replies Tina. "I'll just think ..

Then I'll imagine the way I want to be and maybe say some encouraging things to myself."

"Remember too," adds Mrs. Wood, "that before every lesson you could think of the way you want to act and imagine what it would be like for you to be like that all the time. Feel yourself doing it and let yourself get excited about it."

"Remember you *can* do it and with practice you *will* be able to do it."

The group begin their first week of the goal books.

Every morning before school starts they remind themselves about the way they want to act and they imagine all the people they care about saying nice things about them for doing it.

Good work

well done

That was helpful

You have behaved well

Sometimes Tina finds herself drifting off and Yusuf finds himself starting to speak to the other children but once they realise what is happening they stop and think about what they want to do.

They record each time they're working hard when the bell rings and as time goes by they start to believe they will be able to achieve the goal.

At the end of the day the children count up their ticks and .... Yes! .... Sam and Dionne have got two smiley faces.

Yusuf and Tina have got only one each and both are a little disappointed.

"Never mind," says Mrs. Wood. "Look you both got one smiley face so it shows that you can do it. What do you think went wrong?"

Tina says, "I was dreaming a lot of the time. I didn't realise I did it so often."

"And I was talking," adds Yusuf, "and I didn't know I did it so much either."

"You see," says Mrs. Wood. "That's what these books will show you. They'll help you to become aware of how you behave and that's the first step in changing. Remember you've got lots more chances to reach your targets for the week. Just keep practising and you'll improve. Wait and see."

By the end of the week each child has got the target. Mrs. Wood is delighted and the children are really pleased. They rush home to tell their friends and families.

The children have done what they wanted to do. They have worked hard. The good feelings they have are better than they could have imagined.

Each week the goals change.The next week they try to remember to put up their hands to speak. The week after that they try to stay in their seats, and for the final week they have to do all three things.

They have to get more ticks and more smiley faces each week till in the end they have to get nine out of ten ticks each lesson and nine out of ten tokens each week for a reward.

The rewards change too.

In the second week Sam asks his dad to take him to a football match.

The third week, Dionne asks for a certificate from Mrs. Wood to put in her room. On the fourth week Tina's still too shy to talk about herself but she lets Mrs. Wood say some nice things about the efforts she's made to the whole class.

The children are pleased with themselves. It has been quite hard at times, they've had to think about how they act and they haven't always managed to get every tick or smiley face but the practice has made them a lot better.

"Now" say the children, "See how you can do!"

Section 2 - Application

Procedure for Sessions Weeks   8 - 12

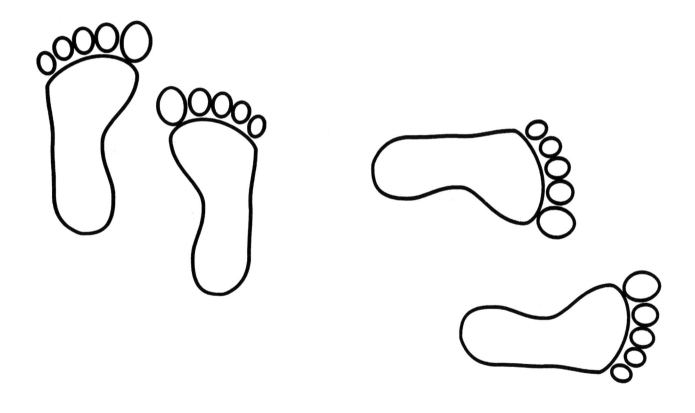

Teacher Notes Procedure for weekly sessions 8 - 12.

Weekly sessions are essential to the success of the intervention. These should be held to review the progress of the previous week and to set goals, targets and rewards for the coming week. Thus, they would be best timetabled for the end or the beginning of the week.

1. Distribution of record books after working on seven stories

In the introductory session give each pupil a record book. These will be used for recording the pupils' behaviour during the intervention. They should be kept carefully and should be brought to each meeting. The four footprints on the front cover represent the steps that lead to the overall goal of the programmme which is self-control. Each footprint stands for one week of the programme, these will be coloured in as weekly goals are achieved.

2. Goal Setting

Open the booklets at the appropriate week. In the large footprint ask the children write the goal for the week. Unless there are strong reasons not to, the first goal should be something common to the whole group. The goal should also be simple so that all the children can carry it out (the first week is largely about getting the pupils to understand what is expected of them). Goals should be expressed in positive terms. Suitable goals for the first week might be; "I can sit in my seat" or "I can work hard". For whichever goal is chosen ask the pupils why it is desirable. Ask them to imagine themselves carrying out the desired behaviour. Model the behaviour if necessary. Ask the children to imagine what it would be like if they reached their targets for the week, how would they feel? What would others say about them?

As the weeks progress the goals should change or become combined with another goal, i.e.,

Week1 - I can sit in my seat.
Week 2 - I can work hard.
Week 3 - I can sit in my seat, and put up my hand to speak.
Week 4 - I can sit in my seat, work hard and put up my hand to speak.

3. Target Setting

As a rule the bell should go off 10 times during an average lesson. Select the number of times in a lesson that the pupil is to be on target during a lesson in order to get a smiley face. The number of ticks necessary should be small and achievable, perhaps 5 to begin with, this can be revised over the following weeks of the intervention, increasing as the children become more adept at practising their skills.

Select the number of smiley faces necessary in the week in order to achieve the goal, again, this should be small to begin with, e.g. 5, rising as the weeks progress and the pupils become more competent.

It is important that all the children should experience success during the first weeks of the intervention so calculate targets carefully.

4. Rewarding

For weeks 1 and 2, rewards should be chosen by the children. It is important they can select what they wish (even though the teacher might not see their appeal) but remind them that they should be kept small. Rewards can include objects, certificates, holding a position of responsibility within the class, for example:

  Peter, 8, chose chewing gum (with parents' consent, to be used outside school).
  Kim, 7, chose a hairband.
  Mark, 8, chose a ball.
  Jamie, 9, chose to do the class messages for a week.

For weeks 3 and 4 greater emphasis should be put on non-material rewards, offering a range of attractive certificates or the choice of a letter home.

When dispensing rewards focus on the pleasant feeling of knowing that the individual has done a good job. Ask the children to describe how this makes them feel.

5. Problems

Problems should be discussed in the weekly sessions. Common problems that arise are often to do with recording behaviour, sometimes children can be over, or under generous when recording on-task behaviour. In cases like these recap on the procedure for monitoring behaviour and clarify if necessary. It will be important here to involve other teachers who work regularly with the class in monitoring the self-recording while the intervention is taking place, explaining inconsistencies if necessary.

Other problems that might arise may be to do with unrealistically high targets. In this case they should be revised to make them more attainable for the individual involved. It is better to err on the side of caution as success can be built on but early failure can make the child disheartened and unwilling to cooperate.

Procedure for Recording Behaviour

The application of self-control skills for on task behaviour should take place during two lessons per day for the duration of the intervention. The aim behind the intervention is allowing the pupils to practise and develop their self-control skills in a systematic manner, this is why it is only practised in selected lessons each day. Once the children have mastered the basic techniques it is hoped that they will apply them to all lessons long after the original intervention has taken place. This effect was noted in previous research.

During the selected lessons a mechanical alarm (kitchen timer) is set to ring a specified number of times at varying intervals. Alternatively an audio tape can be made with 10 bleeps or rings, randomly occurring over a 30 minute time span. This means that the teacher does not have to set the alarm throughout the lesson. Pupils should be warned in advance of the lessons that they will be monitoring their behaviour in.

At each ring of the alarm the pupils should freeze, examine what they are doing and relate it to their target behaviour for that lesson (i.e. whether they are carrying out target behaviours). If their behaviour is on target they should put a tick in the appropriate box in their record books.

For the final week of the programme the method of evaluating behaviour can be varied. Instead of evaluating their behaviour at each ring of the mechanical alarm the pupils could be asked to give an impression of their target behaviour performance at the end of each lesson. If this method is chosen no alarm is used. The pupils can give impression points of meeting target behaviours on a scale from 1-8; 1 representing poor performance of target behaviours and 8 representing very good performance. The class teacher can monitor these impression marks. As with the original procedure, a chosen number of points earns a smiley face for each lesson. The advantage of this is that it encourages the pupils to monitor their own behaviour without reliance upon the intervention materials. In effect the intervention props are being faded out.

The End of the programme

It is advisable to mark the end of the programme with some event designed to highlight the pupils' hard work Perhaps a presentation of certificates of participation in the school assembly could be organised. In addition a display could be constructed consisting of photos of each child with positive comments about their performance on the programme attached. These could be written by the pupils themselves, their classmates or their teacher.

Week _____ My goal is

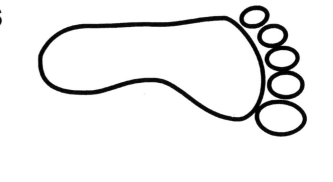

How many ✓ for a 😊 ___
How many 😊 for a reward ___
My reward is.. _____

	Monday	Tuesday	Wednesday	Thursday	Friday
Lesson 1					
Lesson 2					
Success					
Did you get your goal this week?					

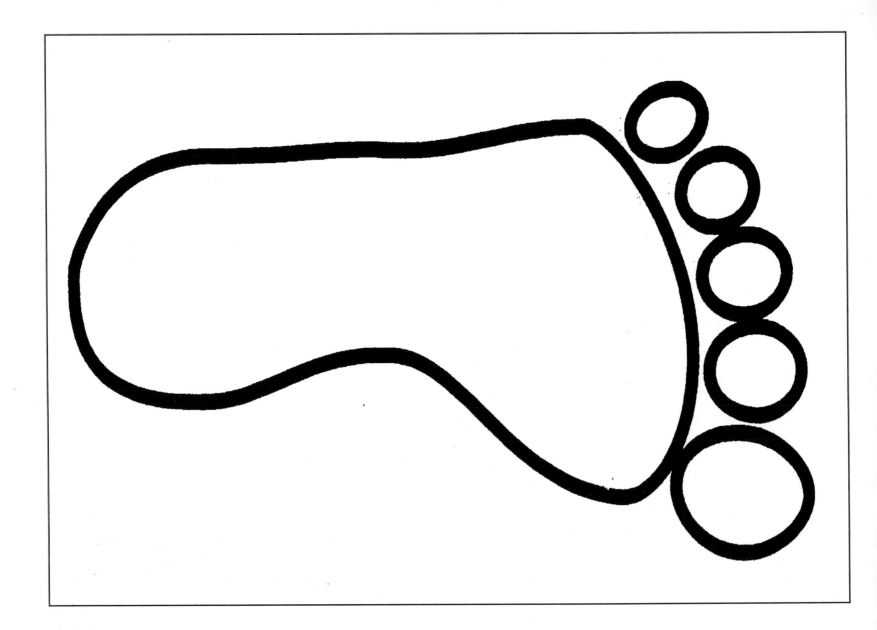